THIS JOURNAL BELONGS TO:

_____

MINI MEMOIR

LONG STORY SHORT

A JOURNAL

BY LISA NOLA

CHRONICLE BOOKS

SAN FRANCISCO

ISBN 978-1-7972-1712-3

Manufactured in China.

Design by Jonathan Glick.
Illustrations by Travis Pietsch.
Typeset in Shady Lady, Berthold Akzidenz Grotesk, and Fazeta.

10 9 8 7 6 5 4 3 2 1

See the full range of Lisa Nola gift products at www.chroniclebooks.com.

Chronicle Books LLC
680 Second Street
San Francisco, California 94107
www.chroniclebooks.com

CONTENTS

INTRODUCTION

Our lives are unique, and our memories are as singular as snowflakes. We all have stories to tell, and that's why memoir writing is for everyone—it is not limited to the notorious or famous. **MINI MEMOIR** is a creative tool kit filled with thought-provoking prompts to help you capture significant stories from your life. Whether you use it to jump-start a creative-writing project or to create a personal keepsake for years to come, this journal will inspire you to engage with elements from your life in an imaginative and thoughtful way.

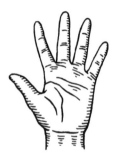

HOW TO

Start with the **LIST FIVE** and create a list of your top five answers.

Then, **PICK ONE** item from your list and delve into it a little deeper with the **FIVE Ws**:

- WHO was there?

- WHAT happened or what significant memory surfaces?

- WHERE were you?

- WHEN did this happen?

- WHY did it happen?

Then, answer the follow-up **REFLECTION** prompt.

Now you're ready to **SPOTLIGHT** that story!

Write about your experience by submerging yourself in the memory and exploring all the details. Think about incorporating metaphors and similes, details from the time period, the five senses, and your takeaway lesson or perspective today.

Above all, be truthful, vulnerable, and brave.
You never know where your **MINI MEMOIR** will take you.

Lisa Nola

Visit LISANOLA.COM
for more inspiration.

LIST FIVE

FAVORITE CHILDHOOD MEMORIES

PICK ONE FROM YOUR LIST ▪ FIVE Ws

WHO, WHAT, WHERE, WHEN, WHY?

REFLECTION
EMOTIONS AND KEY TAKEAWAYS

SPOTLIGHT

SPOTLIGHT

LIST FIVE

MOMENTS WHEN I HAD A CHANGE OF HEART

PICK ONE FROM YOUR LIST ■ FIVE Ws

WHO, WHAT, WHERE, WHEN, WHY?

EMOTIONS AND KEY TAKEAWAYS

SPOTLIGHT

MEMORABLE EXPERIENCES WITH ANIMALS
(pets or in nature)

PICK ONE FROM YOUR LIST ▪ FIVE Ws

WHO, WHAT, WHERE, WHEN, WHY?

EMOTIONS AND KEY TAKEAWAYS

BEST JOB EXPERIENCES

WHO, WHAT, WHERE, WHEN, WHY?

EMOTIONS AND KEY TAKEAWAYS

SPOTLIGHT

WORST JOB EXPERIENCES

PICK ONE FROM YOUR LIST ▪ FIVE Ws

WHO, WHAT, WHERE, WHEN, WHY?

EMOTIONS AND KEY TAKEAWAYS

SPOTLIGHT

MEMORABLE PLACES I'VE SPENT THE NIGHT

WHO, WHAT, WHERE, WHEN, WHY?

EMOTIONS AND KEY TAKEAWAYS

SPOTLIGHT

LIST FIVE

MEMORABLE PEOPLE I'VE LIVED WITH

PICK ONE FROM YOUR LIST ▪ FIVE Ws

WHO, WHAT, WHERE, WHEN, WHY?

EMOTIONS AND KEY TAKEAWAYS

SPOTLIGHT

BEST EXPERIENCES AT GATHERINGS
(parties, dinners, dances, etc.)

PICK ONE FROM YOUR LIST ▪ FIVE Ws

WHO, WHAT, WHERE, WHEN, WHY?

EMOTIONS AND KEY TAKEAWAYS

WORST EXPERIENCES AT GATHERINGS
(parties, dinners, dances, etc.)

WHO, WHAT, WHERE, WHEN, WHY?

EMOTIONS AND KEY TAKEAWAYS

SPOTLIGHT

MEMORABLE FRIENDS FROM CHILDHOOD

PICK ONE FROM YOUR LIST ▪ FIVE Ws

WHO, WHAT, WHERE, WHEN, WHY?

EMOTIONS AND KEY TAKEAWAYS

SPOTLIGHT

SPOTLIGHT

MEMORABLE FRIENDS FROM HIGH SCHOOL

PICK ONE FROM YOUR LIST ▪ FIVE Ws

WHO, WHAT, WHERE, WHEN, WHY?

EMOTIONS AND KEY TAKEAWAYS

SPOTLIGHT

BEST AND/OR WORST EXPERIENCES AT A CONCERT OR LIVE PERFORMANCE

PICK ONE FROM YOUR LIST ▪ FIVE Ws

WHO, WHAT, WHERE, WHEN, WHY?

EMOTIONS AND KEY TAKEAWAYS

INCREDIBLE EXPERIENCES WHILE TRAVELING

PICK ONE FROM YOUR LIST ▪ FIVE Ws

WHO, WHAT, WHERE, WHEN, WHY?

EMOTIONS AND KEY TAKEAWAYS

UNPLEASANT EXPERIENCES WHILE TRAVELING

PICK ONE FROM YOUR LIST ▪ FIVE Ws

WHO, WHAT, WHERE, WHEN, WHY?

EMOTIONS AND KEY TAKEAWAYS

SPOTLIGHT

SIGNIFICANT PEOPLE I HAVE MET AND/OR RECONNECTED WITH

PICK ONE FROM YOUR LIST ▪ FIVE Ws

WHO, WHAT, WHERE, WHEN, WHY?

EMOTIONS AND KEY TAKEAWAYS

SPOTLIGHT

TIMES I'VE VOLUNTEERED AND/OR HELPED SOMEONE OUT

PICK ONE FROM YOUR LIST ▪ FIVE Ws

WHO, WHAT, WHERE, WHEN, WHY?

EMOTIONS AND KEY TAKEAWAYS

NOTABLE INJURIES AND/OR ILLNESSES

WHO, WHAT, WHERE, WHEN, WHY?

EMOTIONS AND KEY TAKEAWAYS

REGRETS

PICK ONE FROM YOUR LIST ▪ FIVE Ws
WHO, WHAT, WHERE, WHEN, WHY?

EMOTIONS AND KEY TAKEAWAYS

SPOTLIGHT

THINGS I'VE BEEN IN TROUBLE FOR

WHO, WHAT, WHERE, WHEN, WHY?

EMOTIONS AND KEY TAKEAWAYS

SPOTLIGHT

TEACHERS AND OTHERS WHO HAVE INSPIRED ME

WHO, WHAT, WHERE, WHEN, WHY?

EMOTIONS AND KEY TAKEAWAYS

SPOTLIGHT

LIST FIVE

MOMENTS WHEN I WAS SCARED

PICK ONE FROM YOUR LIST = FIVE Ws

WHO, WHAT, WHERE, WHEN, WHY?

EMOTIONS AND KEY TAKEAWAYS

SPOTLIGHT

TIMES I'VE BEEN OBSESSED WITH SOMETHING OR SOMEONE

PICK ONE FROM YOUR LIST ■ FIVE Ws

WHO, WHAT, WHERE, WHEN, WHY?

EMOTIONS AND TAKEAWAYS

SPOTLIGHT

SPOTLIGHT

PROUD MOMENTS AND SUCCESSES

WHO, WHAT, WHERE, WHEN, WHY?

EMOTIONS AND KEY TAKEAWAYS

SPOTLIGHT

LIST FIVE

MEMORIES CONNECTED WITH WORKS OF ART
(films, books, paintings, etc.)

PICK ONE FROM YOUR LIST ▪ FIVE Ws

WHO, WHAT, WHERE, WHEN, WHY?

EMOTIONS AND KEY TAKEAWAY

EXPERIENCES WITH COINCIDENCE, LUCK, OR THE PARANORMAL

PICK ONE FROM YOUR LIST ■ FIVE Ws

WHO, WHAT, WHERE, WHEN, WHY?

EMOTIONS AND KEY TAKEAWAYS

SPOTLIGHT

DAYS FROM MY LIFE I WANT TO RELIVE

PICK ONE FROM YOUR LIST ▪ FIVE Ws

WHO, WHAT, WHERE, WHEN, WHY?

EMOTIONS AND KEY TAKEAWAYS

SPOTLIGHT

110

TIMES I NEEDED HELP

WHO, WHAT, WHERE, WHEN, WHY?

EMOTIONS AND KEY TAKEAWAYS

BIGGEST HEARTBREAK MOMENTS

PICK ONE FROM YOUR LIST ▪ FIVE Ws

WHO, WHAT, WHERE, WHEN, WHY?

EMOTIONS AND KEY TAKEAWAYS

SPOTLIGHT

SPOTLIGHT

EMBARRASSING MOMENTS AS AN ADULT

PICK ONE FROM YOUR LIST = FIVE Ws

WHO, WHAT, WHERE, WHEN, WHY?

EMOTIONS AND KEY TAKEAWAYS

SPOTLIGHT

EMBARRASSING MOMENTS AS A KID

PICK ONE FROM YOUR LIST ▪ FIVE Ws

WHO, WHAT, WHERE, WHEN, WHY?

EMOTIONS AND KEY TAKEAWAYS

SPOTLIGHT

TIMES I FELT VULNERABLE OR WORRIED

PICK ONE FROM YOUR LIST ▪ FIVE Ws

WHO, WHAT, WHERE, WHEN, WHY?

EMOTIONS AND KEY TAKEAWAYS

MOMENTS MY CULTURAL BACKGROUND CAME TO THE FOREFRONT

WHO, WHAT, WHERE, WHEN, WHY?

EMOTIONS AND KEY TAKEAWAYS

SPOTLIGHT

SPOTLIGHT

MEMORIES CONNECTED WITH SONGS

PICK ONE FROM YOUR LIST ▪ FIVE Ws

WHO, WHAT, WHERE, WHEN, WHY?

EMOTIONS AND KEY TAKEAWAYS

TOP MEMORIES FROM MY SCHOOL YEARS

PICK ONE FROM YOUR LIST ▪ FIVE Ws

WHO, WHAT, WHERE, WHEN, WHY?

REFLECTION

EMOTIONS AND KEY TAKEAWAYS

SPOTLIGHT

SPOTLIGHT

TOUGHEST EXPERIENCES IN LIFE SO FAR

WHO, WHAT, WHERE, WHEN, WHY?

EMOTIONS AND KEY TAKEAWAYS

MOMENTS I FELT LOST AND/OR LOST SOMETHING

PICK ONE FROM YOUR LIST • FIVE Ws

WHO, WHAT, WHERE, WHEN, WHY?

EMOTIONS AND KEY TAKEAWAYS

MOMENTS MY SKILLS WERE PUT TO THE TEST

WHO, WHAT, WHERE, WHEN, WHY?

EMOTIONS AND KEY TAKEAWAYS

SPOTLIGHT

HARDEST GOODBYES TO PEOPLE AND/OR PLACES

PICK ONE FROM YOUR LIST ▪ FIVE Ws

WHO, WHAT, WHERE, WHEN, WHY?

EMOTIONS AND KEY TAKEAWAYS

SPOTLIGHT

MEMORABLE FOOD EXPERIENCES

PICK ONE FROM YOUR LIST ▪ FIVE Ws

WHO, WHAT, WHERE, WHEN, WHY?

EMOTIONS AND KEY TAKEAWAYS

PEOPLE AND/OR EXPERIENCES THAT PROVIDED ME WITH A NEW PERSPECTIVE

PICK ONE FROM YOUR LIST ▪ FIVE Ws

WHO, WHAT, WHERE, WHEN, WHY?

EMOTIONS AND KEY TAKEAWAYS

SPOTLIGHT

TIMES I'VE LAUGHED AND/OR CRIED THE HARDEST

WHO, WHAT, WHERE, WHEN, WHY?

EMOTIONS AND KEY TAKEAWAYS

TIMES MENTAL AND/OR PHYSICAL HEALTH AFFECTED ME OR SOMEONE NEAR ME

WHO, WHAT, WHERE, WHEN, WHY?

EMOTIONS AND KEY TAKEAWAYS

SPOTLIGHT

MEMORABLE THINGS I DID FOR THE VERY FIRST TIME

PICK ONE FROM YOUR LIST ▪ FIVE Ws

WHO, WHAT, WHERE, WHEN, WHY?

EMOTIONS AND KEY TAKEAWAYS

MEMORABLE THINGS I DID FOR THE VERY LAST TIME

WHO, WHAT, WHERE, WHEN, WHY?

EMOTIONS AND KEY TAKEAWAYS

SPOTLIGHT

TIMES I FELT LIKE AN OUTSIDER AND/OR AN INSIDER

PICK ONE FROM YOUR LIST ▪ FIVE Ws

WHO, WHAT, WHERE, WHEN, WHY?

EMOTIONS AND KEY TAKEAWAYS

TIMES I CONFRONTED AND/OR WAS CONFRONTED BY SOMEONE

WHO, WHAT, WHERE, WHEN, WHY?

EMOTIONS AND KEY TAKEAWAYS

SPOTLIGHT

MOMENTS OF BRAVERY

WHO, WHAT, WHERE, WHEN, WHY?

EMOTIONS AND KEY TAKEAWAYS

SPOTLIGHT

TIMES I CHICKENED OUT

WHO, WHAT, WHERE, WHEN, WHY?

EMOTIONS AND KEY TAKEAWAYS

MEMORABLE EXPERIENCES TIED TO MY GENDER AND/OR SEXUALITY

PICK ONE FROM YOUR LIST ▪ FIVE Ws

WHO, WHAT, WHERE, WHEN, WHY?

EMOTIONS AND KEY TAKEAWAYS

MEMORABLE MOMENTS I INDULGED IN ONE OF THE SEVEN DEADLY SINS (greed, envy, wrath, gluttony, vanity, lust, or sloth)

WHO, WHAT, WHERE, WHEN, WHY?

EMOTIONS AND KEY TAKEAWAYS

SPOTLIGHT

MORTIFYING GROWING-PAINS EXPERIENCES

WHO, WHAT, WHERE, WHEN, WHY?

EMOTIONS AND KEY TAKEAWAYS

MOMENTS I WAS SPIRITUALLY WOUNDED

PICK ONE FROM YOUR LIST ▪ FIVE Ws
WHO, WHAT, WHERE, WHEN, WHY?

EMOTIONS AND KEY TAKEAWAYS

MEMORABLE EXPERIENCES WITH FRIENDS

PICK ONE FROM YOUR LIST = FIVE Ws

WHO, WHAT, WHERE, WHEN, WHY?

EMOTIONS AND KEY TAKEAWAYS

VALUABLE LESSONS I'VE LEARNED

WHO, WHAT, WHERE, WHEN, WHY?

EMOTIONS AND KEY TAKEAWAYS

SPOTLIGHT

MEMORABLE OUTDOOR EXPERIENCES

PICK ONE FROM YOUR LIST ▪ FIVE Ws

WHO, WHAT, WHERE, WHEN, WHY?

EMOTIONS AND KEY TAKEAWAYS

SPOTLIGHT

MOST SPIRITUAL MOMENTS

WHO, WHAT, WHERE, WHEN, WHY?

EMOTIONS AND KEY TAKEAWAYS

SPOTLIGHT

SPOTLIGHT

MEMORIES CONNECTED WITH SMELL

WHO, WHAT, WHERE, WHEN, WHY?

EMOTIONS AND KEY TAKEAWAYS

SPOTLIGHT

MEMORIES CONNECTED WITH TASTE

PICK ONE FROM YOUR LIST ▪ FIVE Ws

WHO, WHAT, WHERE, WHEN, WHY?

EMOTIONS AND KEY TAKEAWAYS

SPOTLIGHT

239

MEMORIES CONNECTED WITH TOUCH

PICK ONE FROM YOUR LIST ▪ FIVE Ws

WHO, WHAT, WHERE, WHEN, WHY?

EMOTIONS AND KEY TAKEAWAYS

SPOTLIGHT

MEMORIES CONNECTED WITH SOUND

WHO, WHAT, WHERE, WHEN, WHY?

EMOTIONS AND KEY TAKEAWAYS

MEMORIES CONNECTED WITH SIGHT

PICK ONE FROM YOUR LIST ▪ FIVE Ws

WHO, WHAT, WHERE, WHEN, WHY?

EMOTIONS AND KEY TAKEAWAYS

LIFE-ALTERING MOMENTS

PICK ONE FROM YOUR LIST ▪ FIVE Ws

WHO, WHAT, WHERE, WHEN, WHY?

EMOTIONS AND KEY TAKEAWAYS

MEMORABLE EXPERIENCES WITH MY IMMEDIATE, CHOSEN, OR EXTENDED FAMILY

PICK ONE FROM YOUR LIST ▪ FIVE Ws

WHO, WHAT, WHERE, WHEN, WHY?

EMOTIONS AND KEY TAKEAWAYS

MOMENTS OF DISAPPOINTMENT OR REJECTION

WHO, WHAT, WHERE, WHEN, WHY?

EMOTIONS AND KEY TAKEAWAYS

SPOTLIGHT

MEMORABLE ROMANTIC MOMENTS WITH SOMEONE AND/OR MYSELF

PICK ONE FROM YOUR LIST ▪ FIVE Ws

WHO, WHAT, WHERE, WHEN, WHY?

EMOTIONS AND KEY TAKEAWAYS

SPOTLIGHT

MOMENTS SOMETHING WENT WRONG OR ALMOST WRONG

WHO, WHAT, WHERE, WHEN, WHY?

EMOTIONS AND KEY TAKEAWAYS

SPOTLIGHT

THINGS I'VE APOLOGIZED FOR

PICK ONE FROM YOUR LIST ■ FIVE Ws

WHO, WHAT, WHERE, WHEN, WHY?

EMOTIONS AND KEY TAKEAWAYS

SPOTLIGHT

THINGS I DESERVE AN APOLOGY FOR

PICK ONE FROM YOUR LIST ▪ FIVE Ws

WHO, WHAT, WHERE, WHEN, WHY?

EMOTIONS AND KEY TAKEAWAYS

TIMES I WAS SURPRISED
OR EXPERIENCED A HAPPY ACCIDENT

PICK ONE FROM YOUR LIST ▪ FIVE Ws

WHO, WHAT, WHERE, WHEN, WHY?

EMOTIONS AND KEY TAKEAWAYS

LIST FIVE

(CREATE OR REPEAT A TOPIC)

PICK ONE FROM YOUR LIST ▪ FIVE Ws

WHO, WHAT, WHERE, WHEN, WHY?

EMOTIONS AND KEY TAKEAWAYS

SPOTLIGHT

SPOTLIGHT